THE WORLD HAS CHANGED FROM WHEN I LAST WAS HERE

Poems by Katherine Mercurio Gotthardt

ISBN: 979-8-9852434-1-3
EISBN: 979-8-3304-0825-2

Virginia, United States services@allthingswritingllc.com

For those who have been victims of broken people,
broken systems.
And for the helpers, in gratitude.

Table of Contents

Umbilical.. 1

Girls School.. 2

Working Order 3

Work from Home 4

Business Trip... 5

Day Job 6

Wing 7

Now That Cuts Are Coming 8

Ivy.. 9

After the Job, the House, Fell Through 10

I Have Learned to Name the Ghosts.. 11

Classic Rock.. 13

Sometimes this is all I need 14

Goldfish 15

BLUF 17

Working Theory 18

Left-Handed 19

Lately 20

Shall I Tell You? 21

First Cousins.. 22

Whatever Gets You Through the Night................................... 23

Heron 24

Letter to Struggling Poets 25

Storyline.. 26

My Dear Friend, the Artist.. 27

Story Telling.. 28

Starting Point... 29

Record Keeping... 30

Cloud Cover 31

Upon Moving Away 32

1969 33

Heritage 34

Last Morning at the Skanky Motel 35

Base Camp 36

Messaging 37

The Last Thing I Drank 38

Haven 39

Drawing Room 40

What the Old Ones Know 41

Larynx 42

Magpie 43

This Poem Is Not for Poets 44

Headlines.. 45

Fallible 46

Delimitation... 47

Predator.. 48

Artistically Speaking 49

Rules for Myself.. 50

Tis the Season... 51

Rebellion 52

Vinyl Village.. 53

Pollinate 54

Reminders 55

Moving Along 56

This We Leave... 57

Poem from a New Home... 58

Revision 59

Persistence.. 60

The Wisdom of Ancient Things........................... 61

Snapdragon.. 62

Eagle Fern 63

Return to Joy 64

World View.. 65

Afterword.. 66

Acknowledgments 68

About the Author.. 69

Umbilical

I was born backwards,
cord wrapped around
my throat, lump on
my neck grown
inward, a daily swallowing
of words, until I learned
I could speak again.

Girls School

Today is, again, a tight uniform,
starched collar around the windpipe
whenever we turn our heads,
rash on our neckline. And there it is,
ruler slap on the desk of
maybe-we-can. Don't you think
to question, girl. Don't you think.

Working Order

We clutch a bit
now for sleep
through the night,
choose sharper tipped
verbs, phrases,
questions of status
quo, but are handed
cliches older than

we are. Blame it
on life change.
On menopause.
Hormones. Bone
loss. Arthritis.
Blame it on
fatigue that

(naturally) wraps
aging in a plaster
cast. Blame
it on the body's
unwillingness
to heal, a fresh

need for stricter
limitation, new
doctor's orders,
reasonable
accommodations,
less time sitting,
standing, more

assistive devices,
larger print, stretching,
a cane, orthotics,
meditation. Do
not think any
of this has to

do with the strain
of being alive
in the same space
as you, thick arms
clamped across
your chest while

you tell us, as
of this morning,
we are no longer
worthy. No longer
needed. Well, we
also have news
for you. Immunity
does not apply here

Work from Home

Impermanence
nothing is actually
owned
lease the day

I learned not to waste
even false promises
dragon lair

perception
paint what you like
to see

riveted to earth
putting nails in our
own
coffin
lying in bed
writing haiku
achoo

Despondence is
avocado toast.
Green backed.
Trendy. Always
on the menu.

Business Trip

1. too-close stranger
   heavy breath on high

2. compartmentalized
   things shift during flight
   ducking

3. acute tilt
   airplane wing and turbulence
   shade shutting

4. no longer possible
   cityscape lights

5. blackened hallways
   carpet schematics and signs
   fallout shelter

6. fire escape
   right outside the window
   casement seal

7. lights always on
   cardigans used as covers
   new night ritual

8. swivel chairs
   statistical foreign
   language

9. one over other
   conversation, pointers
   trick questions

10. hard to chew sandwich
    disappointing lunch

11. bourbon and beer
    everything an import
    unhappy hour

12. only in courtyards
    overpriced salads
    critical greens

13. exhaust
    sole remaining smell
    dead roundabout trees

14. graffiti says
    apocalypse beneath
    rooftop gardens

15. no place to pee
    crusty eyed poodles
    short leashed

16. balanced on railings
    kids in an orange haze
    pigeon walking

17. over an exit
    pedestrians on a bridge
    crossing with pigeons

18. riveted to earth
    driving nails in
    an underpass

19. mourning dove
    calling to a friend

20. too far from home
    wildflower pollen

Day Job

We live in rapid inhale,
the dizziness of trying.
Over-trying. Giving in to
the panic of night sweats,
tachycardia,
an interminable skyline.

We are beings who do not
remember
how to begin.

How to end.

How to be the light.

Wing

there is the difference
they know when to hit high notes
nightingales

speaking in stings
docile nests have few fighters
honeybee homes

are they night silent?
do even their wings find rest?
so much the better

Now That Cuts Are Coming

New year scratches at boardroom windows,
   thin fingered branches. Tenacious.
      Who knows which way the storm
         will take us? We, the remaining leaves,
        determined to outlive winter.

blizzard eye
   each tree limb makes a final request

silencing has its own season
   snowfall whispers

Ivy

For months, we tried to be rid of
you. You, too thick. Too prickly.
Too wandering amid the many
armed hedge and greenery.
Much too, much too, invasive.
And it wasn't for lack of effort
on our part. It merely took some
time. When we finally understood
we could not pry you easily away
with clippers, pliers, curses,

we unpackaged the toxin, convinced,
"This is how to eradicate a nuisance.
Replace it with sapling, flexible,
compliant. Finest of spring shrubbery,
veritable garden." But somewhere
along the way, we splashed that acid
on ourselves during the messy process,
spreading it palm to palm, practiced
fingers coated in a thin layer of
poison, rubbed against obedient leaves

of gardenia we did not intend to burn.
And even now, while we gloat you're
finally gone, we're condemned to look
over shoulders, check daily for stem,
for root perhaps we missed amid the
murder. Sometimes, if honest, while
waking at 4 a.m. to think on our latest
strategy, we wonder if we did

the right thing. Not that we miss you.
Not that we want you back or do
not smirk when we talk about you.
It's more like we look at the price
of herbicide. The cost of carrying
resentment and that little trickle
of sadism into a full blooming war.
We wonder where you'll go next,
where you'll grow again. Was it
really worth it? Well, was it?

After the Job, the House, Fell Through

I would like to tell you that now
I am happy. But I only can tell
you again, a cardinal visited,
spiky headed, depleted from
summer, that it looked inside
and saw the withering of me,
how too often lately, heat from
a cruel noon has suctioned
the essentials: uninterrupted sleep,
nutrients, will. I would mourn

except even that has been extracted, absorbed
where I cannot follow, somewhere between the
cardinal's frail and open wing and the rest of its
mortal body, that space between the space,
through which only breath may pass.

Katherine Mercurio Gotthardt

I Have Learned to Name the Ghosts

In deference to Freddie Mercury and Queen

I have learned to name the ghosts.
Let's call this one Freddie—
no particular reason or relation
to Freddie Mercury, though I do love
a good Queen, especially
when nothing really matters,
and fandangoing now and then,

hair wild as the sun and just as spiky
at the edges, has its advantages over
having to play nice and quiet. I am
not one to take up an instrument,
pick the bones of an old guitar, nor can I
hit the high notes anymore—
that was a me that died a long time ago.
But when I need to turn champion,
having paid my dues again and again,
that's when the spirit takes over,
the way I pretended, as a child,

I had been born a boy instead, told my
mother to chop off my hair, not because I
didn't want to be pretty, but because I didn't
want anyone to pull it repeatedly, and if
some kid had a thing for me, they better buy
me flowers, stop hitting me on the
playground. Because if you think that is
normal, if you still believe "they're just

mean to you because they like you" is okay,
then you are part of the problem, and don't
be surprised when your daughters decide
enough is enough, that they themselves are
enough, and they don't need some version of
the past sneaking up in the brain injury of
night to validate their anger. The present is
plenty reason to go back to the score, the

stomping of music that reminds us we have
committed no crime, that the only infraction
we made was being who we are at this very
moment, and you can't jail someone for
wanting to win occasionally. We don't have

to carry a gun or be the poverty stricken,
unlovable anymore—even the damned have
stood at the stand this time. Even wretched
Beelzebub says we are right. We deserve
better than this.

Classic Rock

Wide eye open, top
of the pyramid scheme,
stairway to some kind
of heaven. Or did you think.
you were self-actualized?
Nah. It's only stone hot

craving, one outrageous
slab upon the shoulders
of another, until we all
are long-dead slaves. Again.

Sometimes this is all I need

Sometimes,
this is all I need:

To sit, secure,
with my palm
on the throat
of day. Press lightly
on its pulse.
Breathe in with it.

Clench.

Loosen.

Unfasten the guessing
of whether it is
innuendo of rain,

or just another wind speaking in
future
tense. Stop being

so yesterday.

So two minutes ago.

So, "This is the start of my
ending." Quit projecting
inhospitable December before I
even get to know autumn.
Rather, write about

black walnuts, released from the
stem. Acorns losing their hats.
The peeling of birch bark. Leaf
fall. Not about their replanting,
or how

everything is eventual recycling,
but about
being okay midair, hovering
between seasons,

between breaths—

within a breath—

living inside the holding of it
and the cradling of myself
in my own well-cared-for
veins. Sometimes,

this is all I need.

This.

Just this.

Goldfish

Once, I killed a fish.

More than once, if you count
the 22 goldfish I accidentally
overfed before the ick took over,
slime around their fins, their mouths,
their boredom, clustering
on their backs until every one of them
rotted within captivity. I swore,
then, I'd never own a fish again,
(as if "owning" a living thing
is an affordable injustice),
the same way I swore
I would never eat something
with a nerve ending.

I was twenty-two that time,
fishing in a little pond, my hook
lodged in the throat of a sunfish.
And though I strived to save it,
grasping it by the neck
the way I'd learned from television
sportsmen, intestines oozed from
its lips, simmered in my hands
while I wrenched the barb out, hoping
to undo the damage I'd done,
confused about where the blood
originated, whether from a being
I hurt, or my fingers sliced by its gills.

The ungodliness of it.

The waste when I threw it back,
hoping it would flop off, splash a bit,
distract the calm of the tight-lipped
basin judging me from the morality of
its own and ancient place. The creature,

abandoned by its school, still bleeding,
lay like a statement, bloated as history,
an unanswered prayer, so dead that,
years later, I still could not look into any
body of water without seeing accusation,
my very reflection having turned

carnivorous, nibbling at the edges of
something more honest with itself,
something very much alive: thin walls of
shared experience, swimming beneath the
same glass sky, the guilty armed with
intention, Others just needing to breathe.

BLUF

Bottom line up front:
There are better ways
to start the day, some
more so than others.
One is by slugging

the alarm clock, uncaring
of mirrors, windows,
happy memories,
and good dreams you
had just had last night,
already forgotten in
the rage your morning.

Another is to wake
gently to the rustling
of your heart, deeply
knowing others awake
alongside you: spouse,
lover, or perhaps warm
furred terriers or tabbies
requesting a beloved
ritual. Spring's

kiss of healthy greens,
practically burst through
the manmade and ridiculous,
things like unnatural schedules
and not enough time
in a day. Too many
tasks to complete
simultaneously—

as opposed to longing
calls of mourning doves,
and the astonishing
wingspan of great
blue heron. Getting
to conclusion, drawing

a crooked line in sand,
perfect synergy of wave
with shore, saltwater
erasing all you think
was ever important:
you are not bespoke
to the digital machine
you yourself set in
last night's darkness.
Rather, you can rise,

quiet blanketed around
you. Make your way to
the door. Open
it to let the dog out,
or perhaps allow in,
hints of tea roses, pink,
in beginning their

bloom. Start over these
critical hours, fresh
in conviction that you now
hear traffic's vagrancy off
in delicious distance,
barely audible. Make

your way back to your
yard of sycamore,
purple rhododendron,
glorious in height,
and nodding—finally
understanding you are

free. You are becoming.
You are your own precious,
early hours, your own
four walls and garden,

and now you need never
go so far away from home.

Working Theory

The theory is this:
If we rage at something
we are not, we become
what we fling ourselves
against, protecting our bodies
from blunt force, active
threat of a tenuous
future. I am here in this
moment in a hyperventilating
hotel, no house, no car
to my name, in my name,
everything held in a cloud,
someone else's server,
even this poem a reminder
we come to the world
with nothing, and we leave it
just the same. And I'd like

to think it is freeing to own
only what I've collected:
shoes and purses, shot glasses,
lapel pins, secondhand
blazers I probably will not wear
again. But even those are stored
elsewhere, others holding them
in accounts I will never be able to
pay for. And if you think I
have chosen this, have taken
a vow of poverty, you will have
thought better of me than I do
of myself, unhappy I judge so
harshly my parts that do not
succeed in systems—
the gilt and splendor I condemn,

because I have known too well
what scarcity means, and I feel it
re-encroaching now, insisting
no one should have to borrow
everything just to survive,
and worth can't be counted
in dollars. I do not believe we are
meant to be empty. Everyone is
a home, everyone deserving of one,
everyone owed their name.

Left-Handed

My left hand has
done most of the work
for me, built a thick
callous on my middle
finger where rests
the pencil's bulk.
Decades ago, when

my desk was smaller,
I accidentally stabbed
my own palm. The mark
is still there, a grey dot,
but barely visible. Even

today, I still manage to
hold the pencil wrong.
And you'd think all my
rings would get in the
way. Not really. At least

not when I write. But
I've been told when I
use my right to shake
someone else's hand,
they hurt. They can
cut you down to the
knuckle. Like a warning.

Lately

And lately,
I seem
seeded
in the same
old place,

lily tongued,
so immensely
in mourning,
in rage, intensely
cyclic, because

I cannot
eradicate
every reminder
of the mobbing,
the infraction,

the fracturing,
no long-stemmed
justice waiting
at the other end.

Shall I Tell You?

Shall I tell you I am disabled?
That I no longer can fend for
myself? Or shall I tell you
I now write the poetry you
mocked me for because
it does not pay the bills?

I'd rather spit sun blaze
into your perfidious eye,
open my onyx robe, expose
the rawness of my words
and show you exactly the way,
as Robin Williams said, they,
and ideas, can change the world.
And while I cannot control how
it all operates—the minute details

of process, decision making, law,
and treachery—I can tell you this:
inside me has turned to oyster shell.
Layer over layer, cemented by sea
and salt. And when you find me
one morning, laying haphazardly
in the sand, you will see my colors,
their gleam and shine and irony—
and you will not think disability.

First Cousins

Perhaps justice
is akin to kindness,
to indigo delphiniums,
cracking their backs
in their reaching,
each hardworking shoot
bending amply for the other,
flexing, allowing in the sun,
reflecting what equity means.

Whatever Gets You Through the Night

And if I have to be transparent,
what has gotten me through
is poetry—the right word
in the right place,
the right memory—
my mother saying,
"It's all part of life,"
even when it should never have been.

Heron

We aren't much to look at, we poets,
unless you look very closely,
(which most aren't wont to do).

It's not that they don't get us.
They just don't have time for us, missing
the chance to observe the heron,

slate feathered, one pencil lead of a leg
secure in the sludge of runoff. The other
raises itself in a mist so opaque,

you can't blame people for hardly seeing it.
To anyone unknowing of creatures like herons,
it would seem it were lacking a limb—

poor amputee in a world where most everything
with power comes in twos, or threes, or more.
Imagine them, then, seeing a bird on one leg

slicing the pool into ripples. Then dipping and raising
its dinosaur head, coming back with the flop of carp,
swallowing the fish entirely, avian throat stretched beyond

what is logically possible by something still
very much alive. So they both remain alive.
We poets. We aren't much to look at. Are we?

Letter to Struggling Poets

My dearest ones, I want to tell you
what I saw today just from looking outside
at the sky: yes, it was grey, and a mist
hovered about the window in shadows
of condensation. And yes, a heavy fog
had been gathering around my heart
for so very, very long, coloring everything
I saw in shades, even the smallest of things,
but today, oh today felt a little like a miracle,
because even though I could not see the sun,
I could see the thin strands of treetops,
still exposed and bare from winter's straight edges,
each of their reaching branches like individual threads,
sewing themselves into the sky, and I recalled

when I used to embroider by hand, my own threads
always too thick inside the hoop, colors bold, unskilled,
abrupt, fingertips sore from trying to force so much through
that thin cloth all at once, and I thought at that moment
what talent it takes for any god to create something beautiful.
And maybe that is why we artists want to make things:

not because we want to be gods, but because we have seen
the hand of something almighty, and we know we are tracing
alongside fingers that do everything by design, and perhaps
that is why it is we, the creators, who feel so very close
to the world, so very much closer to creatures with wings
and spirits – because we are learning to become extensions
of those incomparable places, where immense beauty has been
in hiding within the plainest sight, just waiting to be discovered.

Storyline

After a while,
we get tired of telling
the same story,
the one where we
are interstitial animals
separated by a hand
that decides we are
made to be poor and alone.
And while, yes, creating
means some solitary

confinement, we do want
people to hear us, to see us,
value us the way CEOs,
investment bankers, doctors
and lawyers are graciously
bestowed a livable wage.

But since case law does
not stand behind us,
we keep telling those horrible
tales, the one where artists
cut off their ears simply to
stop the noise, or a writer
swallows a bullet, pulling
the trigger on anything
more they might ever

have written. It is time to
tell a new story, one where
we build our own plotlines,
and unarmed characters
win against antagonists. We
can revise the denouement,

the way the book turns out.
We can illustrate how justice
ought to be. How we ought to be.
Our lives are not on auction.
No one gets a discount.

Katherine Mercurio Gotthardt

My Dear Friend, the Artist

My dear friend,
the artist, while

we have never
really met, I

would like to
say you embolden

me to be more
colorful, more

of myself, bringing
me to where

the water runs
through, deepening

the riverbed, offering
us all a home.

Story Telling

And if you want to know why
I keep telling the story,
it is because
someone else might have lived it,
someone else might need to know,
and when we tell our stories,
in their unprotected truth—
no embellishment needed—
we free ourselves
from what we have been made to carry
on the broken boughs of our backs,
peeling from chaff,
speaking in tongues
that only the honest know,
so some other season,
some warmer, gentler season,
we might actually grow again.

Starting Point

long-tailed and wide-mouthed
three magpies on the front lawn
conjuring the day

Record Keeping

other times
it feels like
not even
the worst what-ifs
can scratch
the too-long awaited
album of silence
on a Sunday morning
in May,
vinyl winged geese
tracking the latest sunrise

Cloud Cover

Still with eyes closed,
wrapped up in blankets
of mammatus, nighttime's
rainstorm having had
the last word, frightening
even our courageous
dog who, usually,
the day after, adores
nosing through blades
to find a tender spirited,
perfect stalk, Sun
decides to sleep in.

It's time, my dear. Go
ahead. Carpe diem, and all.
Rile up the morning.

Upon Moving Away

And I hate to keep mentioning mornings,
but this is the early rising I have waited for,
the one in which the view will be my last,
no more forcing my eye to focus on the few
orphaned trees I have come to so dearly love,
because they, too, seem to have sprung from
nowhere other than tired soil, filling the spaces
where once there was a wood, once there had
been earth children, once there had been native
grandparents and parents of all I consider holy.

1969

Ageism launched the year we
were born—literally. That
was the year they
dispatched us and that
supercharged word into a
no-so-*straight-arrowed*
world. Who knew we would be
accompanied by others,
bonytongued
innuendo, like *chronobiology*,
blind trust, break point,
marginalized,
and *decriminalized*? And then,
the actual history: *"To Be*
Young,

Gifted & Black" premiered in
NYC, while James Earl Ray
finally plead guilty
to murdering MLK. The Viet
Nam war was *nuked* with
blazing protests,
gay rights made a dissidentital
entrance at The Stonewall
Rebellion, and that's
the *tip of the iceberg. Birth*
control pills came legally to
the country, while
Manson, Woodstock, and Nixon
duked out every front page.
This is what we

were *bottle fed* in infancy, as
Merriam Webster
addendumed the dictionary
with expression after idiom,
headhunting new vocabulary
to define a radical

age. How many articulate *Others*
learned early the *jawboning*
progression of
rip-off, high tech,
superconglomerate, sexual
harassment, confidentiality
agreement,
microchip, and *fuzzy logic*? Yet
it's odd—at this
marginalized Gen X
juncture,

we're apparently old,
unknowledgeable. Or
perhaps we all have a *mood*
disorder.
I suppose we could *power*
forward, get our lives
together. Practice *passive*
restraint.
Maybe hire a *life coach.* Or
vinify a garden of
disinterested greenery. Uhm,
yeah. Thanks
but no thanks, not a *parton* of
interest. We'd prefer to
punctuate the market with
zappy brown outs and revolution.
Better watch your step. We
first *walked the moon.*

Heritage

I am back to saying out loud,
nothing is ever one thing –
that in itself a contradiction,
because any time you use
something finite,
something else is singular,
something stands alone.

Let's say everything
is ambivalence, everything
a contrary mix of grapes,
compensatory salt,
and sweetener, the confusion
of living surprise, love,
disappointment, utter
joy and complete devastation—

cocktails of grief and giddiness
in a vessel blown from glass,
handed to us by people
we've never even met,
wondering if we'll shatter.

Last Morning at the Skanky Motel

They say you can't go home again.
That's if you don't have a home,

if your home has closed like a pocket
in the earth, sewn shut by the needling

of inhospitable rain, covered in
loosed clay, gravel, every indication

of an unhappy ending. Nothing is permanent,
my friend. Nothing is ever guaranteed.

Base Camp

panic attack
no address
blanket tent protecting poems

Messaging

Sunday morning.
Persistent cardinal
at the front
window. Tangerine
beaked. High pitched.
Tawny wings
outlined in crimson.
Telling me
it will all work out.

The Last Thing I Drank

The last thing I drank was clear.

The number of times I've had
to repeat this reproduces, every
anesthesiologist preparing for
vomit, I guess. My apologies –

I did not mean to spit that out,
start your day with such a gross
sort of showering, you alongside
me, half naked on a frigid table,
foaming like a geyser's mouth.
I meant to say something more

profound, poetic, give you a
peaceful lake of words,
transparent shallow that,
if you sit still in it long enough
you hardly feel anything but

weightless. Yet everything known
erupts from it: ripples, polliwogs,
mud skippers, algae, iron, and salt,
the much argued primordial ooze
we think long ago might have made
us human. Instead…I'm discussing

puke. But even that comes from
what I last drank, derivative of
placenta and womb, we who are more
than fifty-percent liquid, yet we move
through life like we're solid. As if we're
matter. Like we can't evaporate.

Haven

Finally, silence.
Nothing more than
our original Earth intended.
Where no matter who you are now,
or might have been even a moment ago,
evaporates, reimagined
as fern root, oak leaf, and forest,
cupped in the palm of this accepting sky,
telling you that here,
you have what you've needed.
Here, you have found safety.

Drawing Room

I am wondering
if the ceiling
was touched
by enslaved,
painters from
another country,

another time or
this time, when

agreements like
owning humans
were called
something different,

because we all know
the words we use
matter, the colors
matter, who does
the work matters,

and just because
plaster has smoothed itself
over hundreds of years
in the making,
and no one wrote
the way everything
here went down,

doesn't mean
the inhabitants,
the artisans,
the history,

ever leave
this place alive.

Katherine Mercurio Gotthardt

What the Old Ones Know

And this six o'clock
Saturday morning,
I thought I'd be brave
enough to write about
birds, or how blessed
anyone is to get to grow
old, only I am thinking
about AI, how everyone
is so worried machines
will take over the world,
take over the words,
how it is needless fretting,
as nothing metallic, electric,
or numbered, nothing
that sucks that much
energy from the earth
can ever touch the wing
of our own, dear lives,
each of us in independent
hours, each in our own days
ahead, checking the overcast
sky waiting in line before
just one more hidden sun,
how we all can confidently say
this is not the first shadow
over a daybreak we have ever
seen, not the first scattering
among incoming, hot-breathed
breeze, and no early storm can
possibly carry sufficient lightning
for it to be our last.

Larynx

voice lost
within the stratosphere
thunder seeks the sky

Magpie

My dearly beloveds, I'd like to tell you
and the magpie how very much you are
needed, how very lovely it is to hear you
and your voice, you, arrow-tailed, black-winged,
confident in your sources of innate
knowing, the softness of breast you
reveal in pale patches, unafraid of your
own self and what might next come through
that long-beaked squawk of yours. Do keep on
calling. Please. Keep speaking your truth.

This Poem Is Not for Poets

This poem
is not for poets.

It is for elm,
for juniper,
for fir. For
female fox
and foxgloves.
For ragged-
tailed does
with chances
so scant,
they never
get to see their grandchildren.

This poem
is for nieces,
for sisters, for
mothers, and wives.
For daughters, for partners, for
girlfriends, and lovers … for
those of us holding someone else's
breath whenever a storm
comes on. Whenever news comes
on.

This poem
is not for poets.

It's for solidarity. Camaraderie.
Community. For her,
for you, and now- wombless me.
For sycamore, honeysuckle, for
weeping willow.
It's for we
who share
a name.

Katherine Mercurio Gotthardt

Headlines

It wins a race
against itself
on my bathroom floor,
sliver of a creature,
house centipede
with too many legs,
hairy footed,
creepy in its
coordination, genius
of its own navigation.
It is automation
in miniature,
able to skim
relative miles of tile,
dust, dip, crack,
a marbled plain —
in seconds, a miracle
of self direction.
What a way
to start the day.
Last week sometime,

I read a headline,
in the Times, something
about a three-legged
lion crossing
an African river
of crocodiles —
click here
to find out why.

.

I didn't, caring
only that it succeeded,
that it didn't need
to take some
calculated gamble
we attribute
to other animals,
rather, it knew
itself, understood
what it could
accomplish, and
did. Then
somewhere in
New Zealand,
the transmission
tower that collapsed,
outages skidding across
whole regions
in an infrastructure
fail. Three out of
four of its legs
unbolted, men
and media scurrying
to place blame,
cover up where
possible (as if
dysfunction
so powerful
can be hidden)
no one really

looking at process,
investigation,
how the thing
got there to begin
with, how it came
to be undone.
Meanwhile, an insect

with less than
a raisin brain,
manages hundreds
of legs at once,
and a disabled lion
successfully survives
a river of teeth
and angry hippos.
And here we are, yes?
Tripping over
our own two legs?
Disassembling what
we have built,
unthinking, over-
thinking, dismantling,
falling? Are you
understanding the irony
yet? The oxymoron
of ourselves?
Go ahead and laugh.
There's a bug
running up your pantleg

Fallible

My understanding of dogs is that
they do not make mistakes.
It's more like they misjudge
the way they approach a
middle-aged tabby with unkempt
claws, evolutionarily commanded to
back away from the feral hiss
and swipe that make no sense,
because, isn't that stupid looking
thistle puff with the pointed nose
and oversized whiskers rolling over
to expose its belly? She obviously is
wanting to be prey. Well, isn't she?

Delimitation

My dog watches
squirrels run the fence line,
each outdoing the other,
chattering over
their own antics,
tall tales they are as fast, as innovative, as
they think they are. Unstoppable.

I do not know how she decides
when to rise
on the stiletto of her hind legs,
unnerving in height,
breadth of flexed chest
enough to intimidate
even the uncaring bystander.

Perhaps they should watch their intent.
This time,
she almost has them.

Predator

Getting over myself, I
approach the kitchen sink slowly—

s o o o   s l o w l y,
the blue-tailed skink,

sharp toothed and full
of hereditary stink, sunbathing,

doesn't realize I'm a toe's length
from the thread of its claw,

its hypervigilance,

its brilliance—

millennia of adapting,
surviving, undone by a woman

wielding an empty
cookie jar.

Katherine Mercurio Gotthardt

Artistically Speaking

He asks me why poetry,
especially before coffee.

I should say
the storm — thunder rises
early, alert,

stalwart. I need
not worry, hover
a hand over

its slack lips.
I can affirm: still,
it breathes.

Rules for Myself

Because I did not like your rules,
I wrote some for myself:

Walk outside in new white socks whenever possible.
Pick up pebbles with freshly clad toes.

Let crabgrass try to needle through and hitchhikers
stick to your sole. Stomp as heavily as you wish, delighting

in the pop of spiked milkweed and thistle, rotten quince
and ruminations, helicopter pods spiraling into frenzy

while you collect acorns, black walnuts, the swollen call of crickets.
Pick them all up and slip them next to your skin, right in the cotton cuff,

replacing each tenet that used to confine you simply because
you were born as you were. You are neither label nor thorn,

invasive nor age, not some cliché, prognosis, or pricker, or even
that last red ant in a long line of mischief makers. Reach down

and capture those things that sought to constrain you, make you less
than who you are. Revel in chaos, stacking absolutes into loose piles,

kicking them with cottoned feet, laughing as limitations tumble
alongside everything that never was true, confident you can ingest

the very air you want, exhaling a silk bolt of cerulean sky, or your own
unrestrained storm. Watch with righteous peace as those old codes

fragment and peel, wither and crumble, dissipate into dust
blown mutely back into much more powerful winds.

Tornado. Hurricane.
Mushroom cloud.

Tis the Season

Summertime
Menopause made me do it
Heat of the moment

Rebellion

suburban battle
architecture overgrown
rebellious flowers

Vinyl Village

It is no way to start
the day, one pent
up dog going for
the neck of another,
both at the finality
of their leashes.
On a patch of green

that passes for a yard
stands a tall legged
grill, too close to a
rope of a tree with
roots that have
tied themselves in
knots. Its already
tired leaves bump
against a shredded
privacy fence, rusted
sign tacked to the post,
declaring inherent
right to ownership.
And while we try

to reel them in,
apologizing for bad
behavior, all I can
think of is the last
warm day, how the
smell of meat cooking
had a neighborhood
salivating and tugging
at its primality, all
the wanting having
gone to its head.
The burner must have
been turned on high,
and then, an unexpected
wind. Nothing handy but
fermented iced drinks.
Hazards too close to home.

Pollinate

Daylight has seeped
into a gathering of pollinators,
wings of petal and frond,
no longer ambiguous in predawn,
or weighted by last night's rain, enticed,
instead, by a compassionate skyline,
no longer silent.

Reminders

Thankfully, she, the cardinal,
revisits, only a thin paned window
between me and her reminiscent

chipping. An eidetic sunrise
pours yesterday morning's brew,
full bodied clover topped by mist

and light, reminding me nothing
in this world is truly separate, that
even after bitter, pandemic years,

the softness may yet still return –
we may still return – gentle, purple,
and wise, dappled in experience,

welcoming again translucent winged bees,
the ones we once thought of as everyday,
but now must work to bring back.

Moving Along

Moving inherently means sorting
through the ages, opening trunks

with missing handles, reaching in
deep, pulling out what feels closest.

I was okay until I found her collar,
tags intact, clinking like glass, thin

pieces in opposition, her name,
our old phone number, still visible.

And one hair that had persisted
through years of storage. That one,

single hair. Isn't it funny how tactile
our world is? How terminally memorable?

This We Leave

we leave all this
the way we came in,
sugar maples shedding
their rain from night
storms, drop upon
drop, upon our tired
earth, at once, just
a memory, at once,
its own sort of longing

Poem from a New Home

I don't want to see the news again.
I don't want to know more blood has dumped
from those who have least in their veins.
I just want to hear an overdue summer rain
has splashed the tongue of ageing fawns,
parched for a little kindness. Finally protected
enough to nibble at the edges of native grass.
Of dandelions and thistle. Of cease fire.
Of safety. This is the first love poem
I will ever write from our new home.

Katherine Mercurio Gotthardt

Revision

Now what if
you stopped
panicking
about heat
and the wilted
idea the universe
is doomed, living
is for naught,
and you were
born to destruction?
If on a whim,
on the edge
of a copper
cloud, you bought
penny stock
in hope? Watered
the pollinators
you yourself
raised only
months ago
when you still
had faith
in milkweed,
coneflower,
goldenrod?

I'm not telling
you bury your
face, your good
and loyal mind.
Rather burrow
your fingers,
turned arthritic
on stale keys
into our ample
Earth, soothed in
knowing you loved
it as best you could
at the time. Your time.
Our time. Its time.

Persistence

persistent songbirds
the hopefulness of seedlings
I discover me

The Wisdom of Ancient Things

I return to that Place of Peace,
and the wisdom of ancient things,
the one that reintroduced itself
many years ago, when it was only
me and that ocular moment,
gratifyingly reduced to a single cloud,
stain glass labyrinth wrapping me
in angels' wings. Me, in the kind of silence
where no other words are needed.
Me, before all the old trees had been felled.

Snapdragon

And if you ask me
what it is to age,
I will tell you
what I heard from
snapdragon,
hard words
from such soft spaces:

It doesn't matter what hour it is,
or what you name the day,
what number you assign to
years you have lived
or not. You are likely the same
as half a seed drop ago,
short-lived perennial,
velvet-tongued
as when you called yourself young—
though even then,
it was misnomer,
myth of the regrowing season,
time being what we imagine,
ourselves, a premonition.

Katherine Mercurio Gotthardt

Eagle Fern

In the wondering,
I asked who I am. Not who I might be,

or who I was, one or two
seasons before, but who lives in this,

my fertile moment — now,
when the surprise of a hearty spore descends...

...descends, from an exhausted
frond, shocking the plant itself, poor thing already

thin stemmed, half
confused at where it seems to have rooted. It looks

too shallow, this ration
of clay and sand and stone, not enough for satiety.

Yet, it occurs to me
amidst the falling, amidst the exchange between

ending and beginning,
conversation with blunt winter and a tense summer,

that a shard of glass
also has ground itself into earth, into this evolution

of selfhood. And at this second,
when I feel as both dust and leaf, bleached by the light

of a furious noon and all
we think is holy, I see that, simply, I am. That mostly,

I can exist anywhere. That
I can live here anytime. Mostly, I can be. Mostly, I am the soil.

Return to Joy

wind chimes and songbirds
even the curtains balloon in celebration
today's open window

World View

I want to tell you things look different now,
more early morning, more finch egg blue.

That an undoubting hatchling is still in its shell,
protected by the thin bubble of motherhood,
intact sac separating love from what might

always go awry. And even if it falls, even if
a callous wind brings it to unexpected places,

it will land among softness, handled gently
by field and this, our patient earth. Nested
by sage. By leaf. By lavender.

Afterword

In 2024, the year I wrote these poems, my life had been air dropped into a forest of turmoil. I was managing multiple disabilities. I was forced out of my full-time job. Then my husband retired, and we decided to move out of the hectic, expensive Washington, D.C. metro area.

We tried to sell our townhouse where we had lived for 21 years, only to have the buyers' funding fall through—twice. For several weeks, we were displaced entirely, hopping from one rental to another, collateral damage in a volatile housing market.

We were not the only ones, by far. And at least we had places to stay. Still, I would not care to repeat those months of having to face hostility, instability and fear. I would not care to relive a time that brought back PTSD symptoms I'd experienced earlier in life and now was experiencing again, after enjoying more than a decade without incident.

Thanks to a strong network of capable and caring people, we did manage to relocate to a quieter region in Virginia, for which I am overwhelmingly grateful. I picked up some writing work. I found advocates and support. I am blessed beyond words.

These poems represent part of a chapter, a transition from panic and hopelessness to greater tranquility and reckoning.

I come from humble beginnings. I am of Lebanese and Sicilian descent. A Gen Xer and a first-generation college grad who put herself through school, I have a 30+ year history of writing and publishing. This is my 13th book, in spite of having lifelong disabilities.

I've never been quiet about social justice or human rights. As a 50+ woman with health challenges, I know what it is to be marginalized. To be made to feel less-than. To not have a place, in any sense of the word. To barely scrape by. I know what it can do to a person and how difficult it is to find courage to fight oppressive systems.

Some days, I don't think I have that kind of courage in me. Other days, like today, I feel I am ready, because I am in a place of greater peace—which means, I am in a place of greater personal power.

If you are reading this, and especially if you have lived as "the Other," struggling to survive in a society that does not frequently or warmly welcome differences nor provide easily even basic needs, I hope you know that you do have value far beyond the bottom line. You are just as important as everyone else sharing this planet. You mean something, and so does your life. If you feel you don't, please ask for help. And if you don't know where to start, call or text the 988 crisis hotline.

Thank you for reading this far. Thank you for your time. And thank you for traveling with me. Let's change the world.

Katherine Mercurio Gotthardt, M.Ed.

Acknowledgments

No book is written in a vacuum, nor is poetry.

I have been blessed with inspiration and encouragement from so many loved ones, poets, writers, colleagues, teachers, therapists, doctors and thousands of human beings, many of whom have no idea they influenced or helped me. Below is just a smattering of folks I can credit for this book, individuals and groups that helped me successfully move through a difficult period of my life. Some won't even know why they are on the list. I encourage them to ask.

My apologies in advance for not being able to name everyone.

David Gotthardt
Alexandra Mooney
Andrew Gotthardt
Jonathan Colding
Michael Mercurio
David Lezcano
Jorge de Villasante
Michelle Santos
Vanessa Davis
Craig and Vanessa Gotthardt
Jacki and Lee Prock
Ryan Denny, Realtor
Bill Denny, Realtor
Liz Allen, Realtor
Rebecca Barnes, Publisher
Stacy Shaw, Publisher
Editor Bruce Potter, Publisher
Caiti Quatman, Poet and Publisher

Sheena Mosier, Poet
Anne Morrigan, Poet
Thomas Burson, Poet
@author.taylor.jean
@HaikuFeels
@flip_89db
Victor Rook, Writer, Publisher
Rick Lupert, Poet, Publisher
Satya Robyn, Writer, Buddhist
    Teacher, Psychotherapist
John Berry, LPC
Charlotte Ayuk-Nkem, PMHNP-
    BC
All Poetry – Poets Harbour
    Academy
Write by the Rails/Virginia
    Writers Club
Poetry Super Highway

About the Author

Katherine Mercurio Gotthardt is a Gen X poet of Lebanese and Sicilian descent and a former adult educator serving traditional and incarcerated students. A first-generation college graduate with disabilities, she is the author of 12 other books, including a Silver Award winner from Nonfiction Authors Association, an Amazon bestseller and a Library of Virginia 2024 Literary Awards nominated collection.

Since the early 1990s, Katherine's work has appeared in *Yankee* magazine, *Frogpond, Haight Ashbury Literary Journal, Miracle Monocle's* anthology *You Blew It, Southern Quill, BigCityLit, Haiku Canada, Panoply, Portrait of New England, ONE ART, Poem Alone* and dozens of others. She has won poetry awards from Poetry Society of Virginia, Virginia Writers Club, Loudoun County Library Foundation, Prince William County Poet Laureate Circle, Prince William County Arts Council and various publications. Her poem "Now Entering Manassas" was included in a time capsule as part of the City of Manassas, Virginia's 150th anniversary celebration.

Katherine lives in central Virginia with her husband and their rescue pets. When she is not writing, she enjoys spending time with her grown children, exploring nature and discovering new places in her community. Learn more about her at KatherineGotthardt.com.